The Why Workbook:

A Companion Workbook for

"The Why is the Way"

By

Berta Medina-Garcia

Title: *The Why Workbook: A Companion Workbook for "The Why is the Way"*

Written by: *Berta Medina-Garcia*

Edited by: *Jorge A. Garcia, Jr.*

Website: *www.dreamerssucceed.com*

Copyright © 2018 by Berta C. Garcia / Dreamers Succeed Publishing, LLC, a Florida Limited Liability Company

ISBN – 978-0-9861221-2-5

INTRODUCTION

Self-improvement is not easy. It was never supposed to be. Ask anyone who has improved their life in some significant way. You will hear an echo. "It was hard work."

Anyone who says it was easy is just trying to sell you something. Anyone who says it was simple is half-right.

The reason improving ourselves is so hard lies in the chasm between our thoughts and behaviors. We can be receptive to all our greatness and believe in our future, but it means literally nothing if we're not taking the action required to "do the damn thing."

Change isn't just about seeing life in a new way. It's about using that new way to do things with the body and brain you were gifted.

When we don't take action with our positive energy, we deflate. We wonder why things didn't change when we used our affirmations every single day. We curse our colored parachutes for not accurately depicting what we ought to do with our lives. We never look at the root cause of our misery: our assumption that changing our thinking changes our lives.

To know that you are great means nothing if you don't behave like it. To understand what's holding you back won't help if you don't push forward. The war wages on against toxic habits. We may be inspired at first when we read the latest self-improvement book or hear an exciting and motivating speech, but the high of optimism rarely lasts.

Where you change your life for the better is in the actions you take with that power surge. Reading about improving yourself is easy. It releases endorphins and makes you feel as if you've actually accomplished something.

"Now I know the *real* answer to how I can improve my life."

There is no real answer. Everyone's got different answers that are equally effective. Many of them work if you actually use them. Very rarely is one more *real* than the other. But we struggle and subscribe to newsletters and blogs and purchase the next best book in hopes that we find the "right" answer.

The right answer that we're often looking for is the *easy* one. It's the one that'll take no work at all. That's what we truly desire -- a fix-all for our happiness and lives that will completely change everything by just *reading a book*. If only!

I, myself, have been guilty of reading the latest self-help books for kicks and kicks alone. I'm sometimes arrogant enough to wonder why they're not working for me.

100% of the time, it's that I'm not working for them.

You can't just take a current and pray it reaches the bulb. You must use a conduit to ensure that it doesn't arc haphazardly. The wire or conduit contains and directs the energy. Hopefully, this workbook will serve as the wire that guides your energy to the things you truly desire.

I wrote this workbook as a companion to *The Why is the Way*. Though I believe the book stands on its own, there are some who would benefit from being guided by a sort of "coach on the page" to discover what it is they really want out of life. With the context of *The Why is the Way*, many of these questions will hopefully hold some meaning for you and correlate to the chapters in that larger work.

The concepts are loosely related and don't rely *too* much on that content, so fret not if you haven't had the chance to read the book that inspired this one. If you *do* want more info or to get some context on what you're reading, you can find The Why is the Way on Amazon.com, available in print or kindle editions.

What follows here are exercises that will assist you in forming mental and behavioral habits that will get you where you are inspired to be. Follow the exercises and do them. Don't just read them.

Follow along, stay inspired, and good luck on your journey. Enjoy the process.

MODULE 1 - DEFINE THE WHO

If you want to be the best version of yourself, figuring out who you are is the first step.

That's a deceptively simple question, isn't it? "Who are you?" Here's a challenge: what if you couldn't answer with your name or your occupation? What happens then? Who do you *become*?

We don't often expect an inquiry that profound to come up in daily life. On top of that, we often (and honestly) believe the mask we wear is who we actually are.

As a coach, I ask people who they are *all* the time. 98% of the time, a person will jump right in to tell me what they do for a living. Not quite what I'm looking for, but I totally understand why the question gets misconstrued. That's often what people really mean when they ask you who you are. They want to know how you make your living and what position you hold in society.

I used to be in that 98% myself. The other 2% of the time, they will either squint, stuck in thought, or offer me a deer-in-the-headlights silence.

The bottom line to all of this is that we are human beings, not human doings. This module is designed to help you answer this tough question with confidence. And having that answer isn't for the sake of telling other people who you are. It's about having a definitive answer for every time you ever doubt yourself, you wonder what your motivations are, or you wonder where you're heading in life.

In addition to setting a foundation for your goals and personal triumphs, you'll also be more content. When you live in line with who you actually are instead of what you think you ought to be, happiness is a constant companion. You'll be a better decision-maker, have more self-control and be much more tolerant and understanding of others. Additionally, you will find that life overall becomes more enjoyable.

As promised, in this module you're going to have a chat with yourself, digging deep to get to the uncomfortable stuff. This will be essential and without this experience and practice, you will not have the foundational knowledge you need to move forward – plain and simple.

As I mentioned earlier, if this module is easy, you may be doing it wrong. You have to be honest with yourself. This is the part where you sit down and face the things you're always ignoring; where that inner voice finally gets to speak its piece.

Please make some space for yourself, physically, mentally and emotionally to complete these Transformation Exercises.

Start this module by asking yourself – WHO AM I?

My Journey to Self-Discovery

Transformation Exercise 1:1

Your Story Today

In narrative form, write a brief story of who you believe you are. If you prefer, you can also give a dictionary definition of yourself. Think about it, if your name and photograph were in the dictionary, what would the definition next to you say? Include personality traits, hobbies, and passions.

_____

_____

_____

_____

_____

_____

_____

_____

_____

_____

_____

_____

_____

Transformation Exercise 1:2

Who Are You?

The following questions will help you uncover a great deal about WHO YOU ARE. Please keep an open mind, as these questions are designed to generate more questions you will come up with on your own.

Please don't feel confined to space when answering these questions. Make sure you are writing down the questions that are coming up for you as you respond to these. Most importantly, ponder on your answers. Are they revealing anything to you that you might not have known before or perhaps knew but had forgotten? If so, great! If not, go back and re-do this exercise. Underline important findings, add commentary, and be observant. You might be surprised what a second attempt can reveal.

What or who would you be if you knew you couldn't fail?

The risk of failure can be paralyzing for some people. Imagine you had a 100% guarantee that you couldn't fail: what or who would you be?

What are your core values?

Have you ever heard someone say 'if you don't stand for something you'll fall for anything'? Well, what do you stand for? What principles do you try to live by, whether consciously or unconsciously.

How would you describe yourself to someone meeting you for the first time?

Resist the temptation to mention anything about what you do for a living. Exception: if what you do for a living brings you so much joy and is in alignment with what you truly want, definitely include it but focus on personal traits more so than the work you do.

What makes you genuinely happy? What activities do you take part in that make you smile? What never feels like a chore?

_____

_____

_____

_____

_____

_____

_____

_____

_____

_____

What have been some of your biggest challenges and how did you overcome them?

_____

_____

_____

_____

_____

_____

_____

What are you most proud of in your life?

What are your talents?

(Specifically, what physical things are you good at).

What are your strengths?
(What emotional, mental, or physical traits do you excel in?)

What do you love most about yourself?

**What have you accomplished that
took the most courage to accomplish?**

What makes you feel most alive? What gives you a rush?

Transformation Exercise 1:3

Finding Your Core

You may have at some point seen or heard of Russian Nesting Dolls also known as Matryoshka. They're often times ovular wooden dolls which, when you open them, reveal another, smaller doll inside. Then you open that one and discover there's yet another version of the same doll. And so on, and so on. We're like those nesting dolls. There are a whole lot of layers to our humanity. Our exterior layer is the one the entire world sees. For most of us, that is the one we feel safest showing.

The next layer is the one we are to most of our acquaintances or people we don't know on an intimate level. The next layer is probably who we are to our friends and business colleagues. The next one may be who we are to our closest friends and relatives. The next one is who we are when we're alone -- when there's no one to impress or put on an act for. That's the most central doll in the Matryoshka. It's small, but its size betrays its power. It's the heart of everything. The smallest doll can't be undone. This is the core of who you are – your CENTER.

This version of you is who we want to find. It's the person that you really are -- the one that deserves to be free. Connecting with your core can bring up memories and emotions that are key to revealing the truest version of yourself.

Think back to when you were a child, before you were 5 years old, let's say. If you don't have great recollection, find pictures of yourself and see what you were doing? What were your facial expressions? What did you love when you were a young child? We are our truest selves as young children before we begin to accept all the limiting beliefs we are fed by our parents, families, society and the world.

So, what did you discover?

Transformation Exercise 1:4

Digging Deeper

Now that you've done a bit of digging and had some time to explore these first few exercises, here are a few more questions to help you continue to peel back those layers.

An activity in my life that lights me up with pure joy is:

I believe it's possible for me to:

I believe that humanity has changed for the better by my being here because:

People perceive me as:

_____

_____

_____

_____

_____

I find this to be true no matter what:

_____

_____

_____

_____

_____

I believe the meaning of my life is:

_____

_____

_____

_____

_____

_____

_____

Transformation Exercise 1:5

Finding Your Strengths

One of the most transformative aspects of self-discovery is recognizing your strengths and talents. Trust that they are there and trust that you have an abundance of strengths and talents that you may not even be aware of, not consciously anyway. Take your time answering these questions and if they spark other questions of your own, write those down and answer them as well. Remember to be inquisitive.

Three of my greatest strengths are:

_____

_____

_____

_____

_____

_____

The very first achievement I can remember is:

_____

_____

_____

_____

_____

What I like most about myself is:

_____

_____

_____

_____

_____

Some unusual skills I have are:

_____

_____

_____

_____

_____

My greatest talents are:

_____

_____

_____

_____

_____

Transformation Exercise 1:6

My Story

In narrative form, write the story of who you are today. No limitations, physical, mental or spiritual. (You may need extra pages – go for it!)

_____

_____

_____

_____

_____

_____

_____

_____

_____

_____

_____

_____

_____

_____

_____

_____

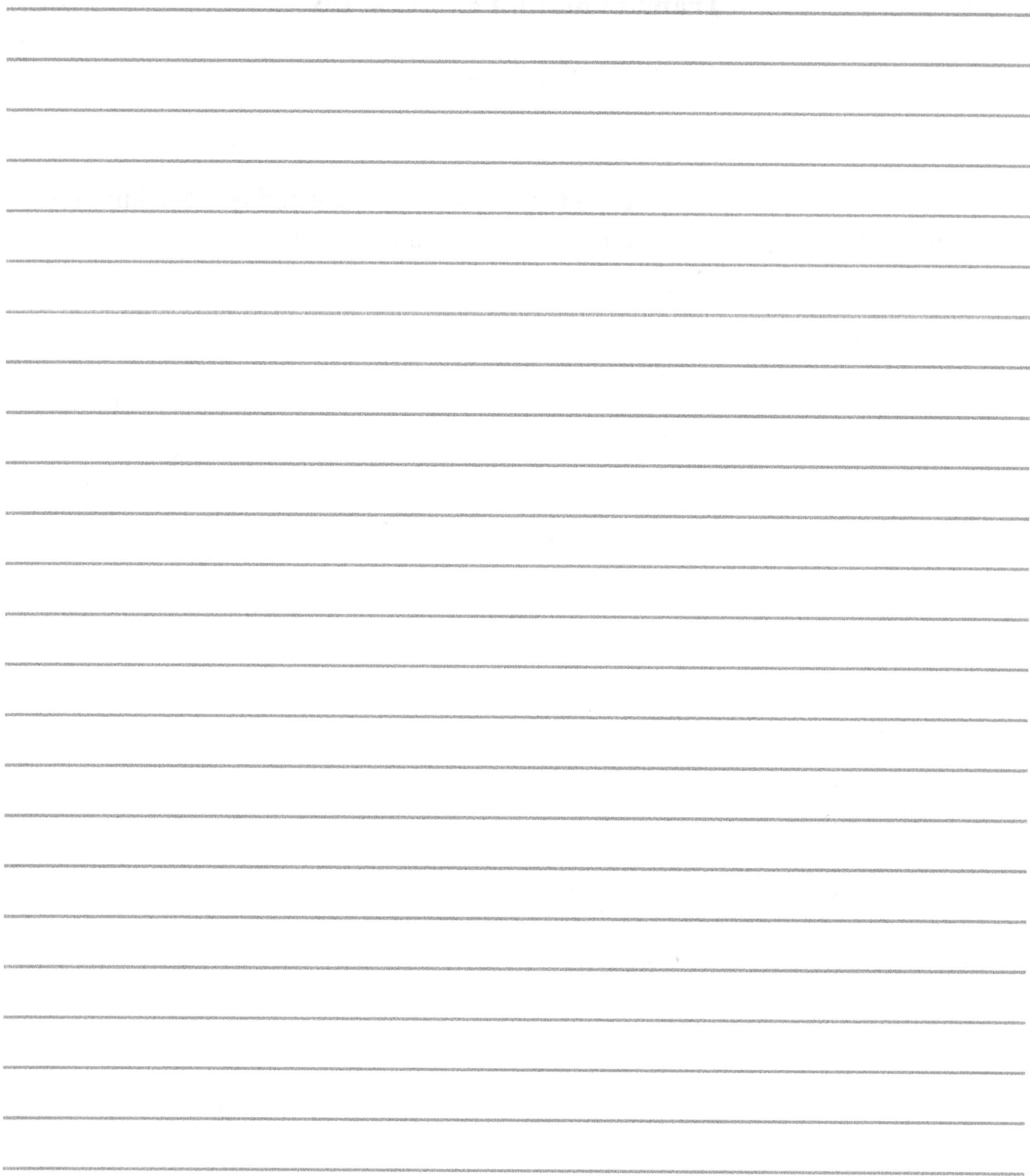

MODULE 2 –DEFINE THE WHY

Besides the fact that achieving our dreams takes hard work and dedication, there's one other (surprisingly common) problem to tackle. Sometimes, we don't even know what our dreams or passions are in the first place.

If someone asked you, "What do you want to do with your life?" would you have an answer prepared? Can you condense it into a few clear sentences, no "ums" or long pauses? Most importantly: does the question bring you joy (as opposed to anxiety)?

If you haven't nailed down the definitive answers, don't worry – you're not alone. In fact, the majority of us are just trying to keep our heads above water with our jobs, home life, and relationships. It's hard to focus on what we desire when we're all trying to get what we need. But life is a balancing act, and you're going to learn how to include your dreams in your day to day.

In this module, you'll explore and uncover dreams and passions you've simply never bothered writing down. Hopefully, you'll also rediscover the ones you've forgotten about.

As with the previous module, you'll be answering some questions here that, once again, will trigger other questions. This is not a race, so take your time with the questions. The more effort you put into each, the better your results. Answer these questions honestly and without straining yourself. Let it come from a place of confidence and don't second-guess anything. Typically your first answer is your best answer and remember, there is no limit – no ceiling - the bigger and greater your passions the better.

If you feel like it would help, go through the questions again after a day or two and re-answer them. If the answers change, that's fine, that's part of the process. For this module, ask "What are my dreams? What am I truly passionate about?"

Transformation Exercise 2:1

Where are you today?

In list form, write down some of your dreams (goals) you have. Focus on the ones that come right to the surface, the ones that you can't deny. Write down what you're passionate about. If your list is longer than what you can accommodate on this sheet, write on the back or in a notebook or anywhere. Just make absolutely sure you get your thoughts on paper.

1

2

3

4

5

6

7

8

9

10

11

12

13

14

15

16

17

18

19

20

Transformation Exercise 2:2

Let's Explore

Answer the following questions with the first answer that pops into your mind. If you feel you'd like to change it later, I'm going to ask you for this segment to please avoid doing that. Remember, there are no limitations here – you are answering as if failure was not an issue or an option (because it isn't):

What do you love to do?

_____

_____

_____

_____

_____

What would living your life to the fullest look like?

_____

_____

_____

_____

_____

_____

_____

_____

_____

**If you were living the life of your dreams already,
what would your calendar look like this week?**

_____

_____

_____

_____

_____

_____

_____

_____

What excites and inspires you?

_____

_____

_____

_____

**How can you use your strengths, skills,
and inspirations to lead a better life?**

_____

_____

_____

_____

_____

_____

_____

_____

If you took your time with these and answered honestly you should have a new level of clarity. Writing things down helps us form stronger memories and reinforce ideas. What's especially important is that now you'll have specific, concrete "evidence" of what you want most that you can come back and refer to.

Sometimes, we're not willing to admit what we truly want because we're scared of failing or being rejected. When push comes to shove, we fool ourselves by pretending our goals never existed, assuring ourselves that we're perfectly happy where we are now.

If you have a gut feeling you didn't answer all the questions honestly: follow it. The benefits you get from this exercise are proportional to how honest you are with your answers. Scrap this and redo it until you feel like there's nothing left to say.

Transformation Exercise 2:3

Let's Evaluate

Now that you've had an opportunity to explore a bit into your dreams and what you're passionate about, please go back to that narrative you completed in your final exercise of Module 1. Do you see any overlaps? Would your answers to these questions resonate with your story?

_____

_____

_____

_____

_____

_____

_____

_____

_____

_____

_____

_____

_____

_____

_____

Transformation Exercise 2:4

The miracle of YOU?

You are a miracle – did you know that? YOU ARE A MIRACLE.

Dr. Ali Binazir, "Happiness Engineer," agrees. We can move in reverse through your timeline and you'd quickly see how incredible your existence is. The fact that you were born in the first place, then going back to your parents, grandparents and everyone down the family tree, considering wars, famine and every other factor that could have gone wrong to keep you from existing. That's a whole lot of factors.

His study found that the chances of you existing are 1 in 500 squintillion. Did you even know that existed? I didn't.

Here's a more down-to-earth analogy for how unlikely that is: 2.5 million people to play a game of dice with each dice having a trillion sides and they all have to roll the same number. It's so unlikely that it's almost impossible, but that's how much of a miracle you are.

You are wholly unique. I'm not saying it to make you feel all warm and fuzzy. Factually speaking, the odds that you're here are SIGNIFICANTLY LESS THAN 1 in 500,000,000,000,000,000,000. I'm not going to dispute the math here. That's pretty dang unique.

You are here for a reason. Even if it's not completely clear, those astronomical odds paint a very convincing picture. Webster's defines purpose as "the reason for which something is done or created or for which something exists." Why is this important? Because very often your purpose and your passion are the same things.

Do you remember the first time you questioned why you were here? What your purpose was? That's a significant moment in our development as intelligent and spiritual beings.

Do you remember the first time you felt that something you were doing was so true to your being that it made you feel more alive than anything else? Chances are, you were doing or going through something at the time that was in alignment with your purpose.

Can you elaborate on that a bit?

(If you can't quite get an answer yet, no worries, not everyone has experienced this... at least not on a conscious level.)

_____

_____

_____

_____

_____

_____

_____

_____

_____

Regardless of anything you may or may not have completed just above, if you had to guess what your purpose was in this world, what could that be?

_____

_____

_____

_____

_____

_____

_____

Transformation Exercise 2:5

Quest for Purpose

This QUEST FOR PURPOSE is an exercise to help you discover your life's purpose. Your great purpose or dreams in life are usually wrapped around or directly correlated with your great passions. However, as you may have already discovered, knowing what your passions are may require some digging. This exercise will help unearth some of your most fulfilling passions. Many times, they're buried deep under limiting beliefs, fear, negative programming, old wounds, criticisms, etc.

Give yourself at least 20 minutes to complete this exercise -- take more time if needed. This initial portion of the exercise should be completed in one sitting so please wait until you have the time to dedicate to it. Also, I recommend that you get to a quiet environment, free of any distractions.

Make a list of 25 things you feel most passionate about, dreams you've always wanted to accomplish. Do not hold back or over-think. Go with your gut, usually your initial answers are the best. Do not censor yourself, make your list of dreams as big as possible – remember nothing is impossible!!!

Make your statements clear, short and sweet. Don't combine. List each thought separately. Don't be afraid of what's revealed on the page. This is your quest and no one else is going to read this unless you want them to.

Tip: If you are not able to readily come up with this list, try asking yourself the following questions based on you living your ideal life, "Who are you?"; "What are you doing?"; "Who are you with?"; "Who are you serving?" "What do you have?" and any other questions which may be triggered by these questions:

1

2

3

4

5

6

7

8

9

10

11

12

13

14

15

16

17

18

19

20

21

22

23

24

25

I hope you are enjoying this process and that these answers are bringing you joy– they should be, after all, these are your passions.

Now, please put this list somewhere and come back to it tomorrow.

Once you've had about 24 hours to let this simmer, please go back and peruse your list as you're going to be narrowing down a bit.

QUEST PART II: MY REGROUP

During the next step of this exercise, you will be narrowing this down. Since there are (or may be) 25 items, let's regroup them into 5 sets of five. For example, Take 1 – 5 in one group; 6 – 10 in the other; 11 – 15 in another; 16 – 20 in the next; and finally 21 – 25.

Here's what you're going to do: Take statements 1 – 5. Does what you wrote for Number 1 resonate more for your than what your wrote for Number 2? You will keep one or the other. Once one of these is preferred, the not-chosen one is out of 'play' if you will. Then compare 1 to 3. Which one of these stays? 1? Okay, then do 1 and 4 – which one stays of these? 4? Then do 4 and 5. Get it?

Once one of your choices in each group eliminates all the others, this one gets added to the A list. The other 4 are going to a B list. The point of this exercise is to come up with 2 lists: Your A list will have 5 items in it and your B list will have 20 items.

You will then take your B list and without breaking them up into groups, you will repeat the process of elimination to come up with your top 10 from there. In other words, you will eliminate until the top 10 from this list are known.

A List:

1

_____

2

_____

3

_____

4

_____

5

_____

B list top 20:

1

2

3

4

5

6

7

8

9

10

11

12

13

14

15

16

17

18

19

20

B list top 10:

1

2

3

4

5

6

7

8

9

10

QUEST PART III: MY TOP 7 PASSIONS

So at this point, you have 5 items in your A list and 10 in your B list. Now you will go down the list, without separating them or categorizing them. Once again, go through this process of elimination starting with the 5 from your A list above the 10 from your B list. Remember, the point of this last section is to come up with your 7 top dreams and your true purpose will be revealed – the things that matter most to you.

Why 7? The number 7 is a number that represents and has been known to signify completeness and perfection. Having said that this is YOUR QUEST, no one else's. If you would rather have a top 5 or a top 3, feel free to tweak this to work for you because after all, this is to help you focus on your true passions and dreams.

My passions list:

1

2

3

4

5

6

7

TRANSFORMATION EXERCISE 2:6

My Passions

In narrative form, write the story of who you are when you're living with passion. There are no limitations whether physical, mental or spiritual.

MODULE 3 – DEFINE THE WHY NOT

Are you ready to talk about your thoughts?

I don't want to get too metaphysical here, but all of your experiences are direct products of your thinking. I don't mean to say that you can manipulate the world with your thoughts. What I mean is that your thoughts give you perspective, form your emotions, and have an impact on every action you take.

This is your story and you are the storyteller. The world around us often feels like it's happening to us, but when we take responsibility and choose to change things, suddenly it's happening with us. It's in our nature to project our thoughts onto the world around us. That's why some people shrink away when tragedy strikes ("the world is against us") and others grow from it ("I've learned a valuable lesson through this").

Have you ever heard the saying "As a man thinketh in his heart (or his mind) so is he?" Think about that statement. That statement from the book of Proverbs in The Bible is a difficult one to have avoided over the course of your life.

I want you to repeat that saying to yourself. Slowly. As a man or woman thinketh, so is he or she.

The best lessons in life we learn the hard way. Take it from me, who experienced life just as I'd envisioned it year after year, wondering why I wasn't getting where I wanted to go.

Your life is traveling at the speed of your thoughts. I envisioned life the way it was, which is exactly what it gave me in return. Your life, whatever that looks like for you today, is first created in your mind, then in your world.

This is going to be a busy module, but you're going to be peeling away some very complex "stories" you tell yourself.

For this module ask yourself "Are my thoughts in alignment with the life I want to live?"

Transformation Exercise 3:1

Your Thoughts

It's time to take a look at the life you're currently living and pinpoint the thoughts that are making it so. In order to do this, please take your time answering the following questions. Just pondering on and answering these questions will reveal a great deal about what's really going on in your life behind the scenes. By the time you finish this questionnaire, you'll be finding lots of connections and answers that were totally "invisible" to you before.

Do your default thoughts tend to be more positive or negative in nature?

_____

_____

_____

_____

_____

What is "the truth?"

_____

_____

_____

_____

_____

What makes you who you are?

_____

_____

_____

_____

_____

_____

_____

_____

How do you know your perceptions are real?

_____

_____

_____

_____

_____

What things hold you back from doing the things you want?

_____

_____

_____

_____

_____

Where do thoughts come from?

What is emotion?

What is doubt?

How do you define fear?

Transformation Exercise 3:2

Are you Limiting Yourself?

You're already everything you ever wanted to be. It may not look like it from the outside, where the situation doesn't match up with what you want. But you, as a person, are already who you dream of being.

The problem is that you can't see yourself under all that mess of limiting beliefs, doubts, and fears. Once you chisel everything away and reveal that real you, living your exceptional life is guaranteed!

Your road in life is determined by your beliefs; if they're limiting, your road is going to be mighty narrow. The sooner you dispel those limiting beliefs, the better. But you have to figure out just what those are. It's not as easy as just believing in yourself. It's about disbelieving the negative narrative you've been selling yourself.

If you had to identify some of your limiting beliefs, what would they be?

_____

_____

_____

_____

_____

Where did these beliefs come from?

_____

_____

_____

_____
_____
_____

Did people give you these beliefs?

_____
_____
_____
_____
_____

What is a lack in belief in yourself costing you?

_____
_____
_____
_____

Where do you think your thoughts could be getting in the way?

_____
_____
_____
_____

Where are you too hard on yourself? (Make a list)

I should always...

I should never...

Where in your body do you feel stuck or held back?

_____

_____

_____

_____

What holds you back?

_____

_____

_____

_____

What is the positive intention of holding
on to some of these limiting beliefs?

_____

_____

_____

_____

_____

Is it useful for you to continue believing these thoughts?

_____

_____

_____

_____

What concrete evidence do you have to back up any of your limiting beliefs?

_____

_____

_____

_____

Write a narrative of everything that must be removed for you to journey into who you need to become to live that life.

_____

_____

_____

_____

_____

_____

_____

Transformation Exercise 3:3

Thoughts and Limitations

You have now been able to dig a bit into your thoughts and how some of them may be limiting you. Based on the answers and discoveries of the previous two exercises, do you see a pattern or any correlations? This may or may not be the case however, if there are, please explore them.

Are there any correlations between your findings here and what you've discovered in Modules 1 and 2? Review your findings through the modules thus far.

Write down a narrative of any overlaps you have found throughout all the modules you've completed so far.

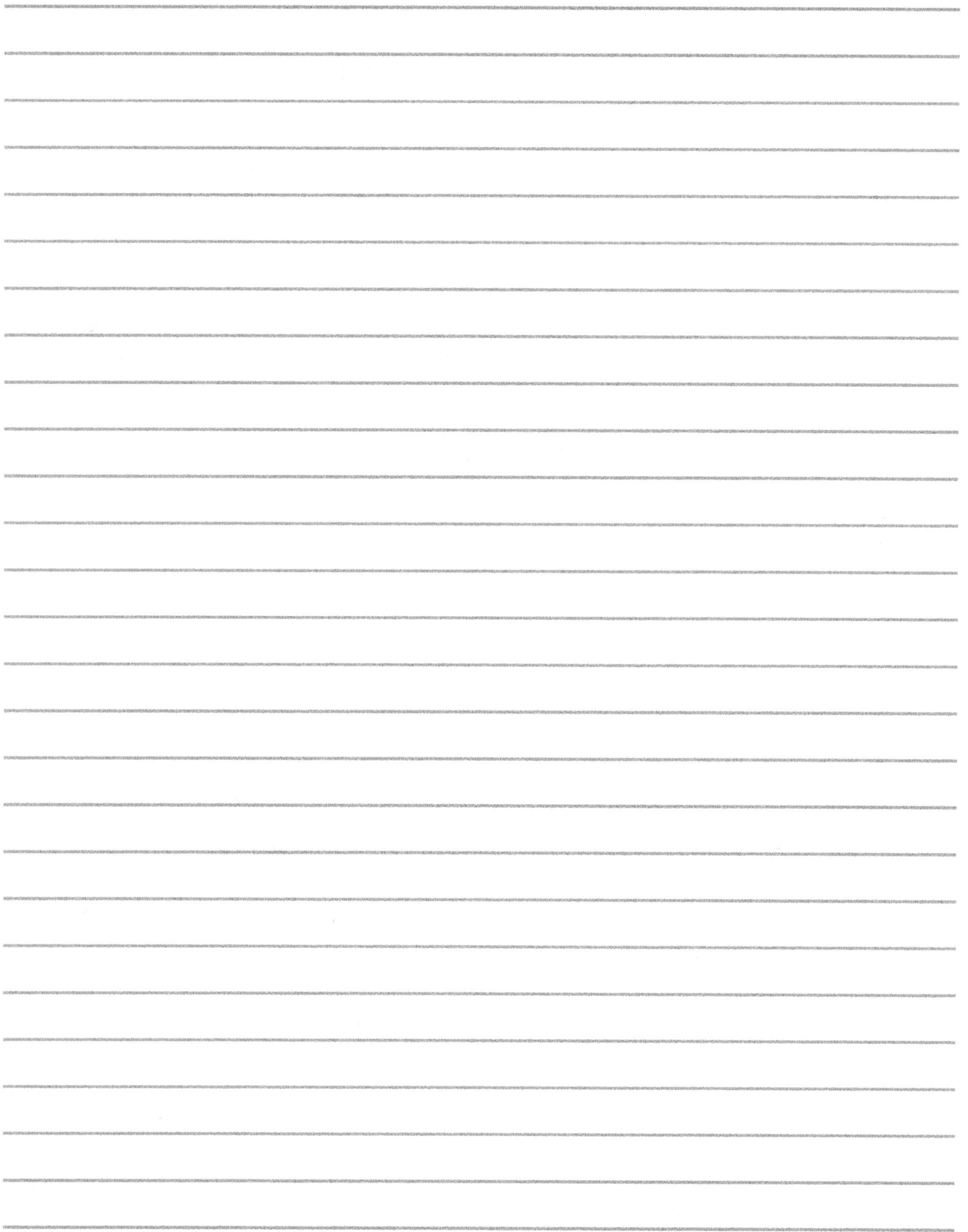

Transformation Exercise 3:4

Fears to Leave Behind

Fear only exists in your mind – it doesn't exist or live anywhere else. Do you know that we humans are only born with two fears – the fear of loud noises and the fear of falling? THAT'S IT! All our other fears are instilled in us by society, our experiences, our parents, teachers, even our DNA. Some of these fears are healthy (you shouldn't be petting every snake you see), but many of them are irrational and totally emotional.

You'll be discovering ways to uncover and dispel these fears you are holding on to.

I'll give you a brief example of these inherited fears (or unfears in this case). My Mom, at 82 years of age, is still afraid of the dark. When I was a wee little girl, barely walking and newly potty trained, it wasn't unusual for me to need to tinkle in the middle of the night.

The bathroom was in the hall where turning on the lights caused half of the family of 8 living in this 2-bedroom apartment to be awakened by a light in the hall. My Mom would encourage me, at not quite 2 years old, not to be afraid of the dark – to go ahead on my own.

Of course, she was giving herself an "out" from having to venture into the dark hallway. With this habit, she accidentally instilled a sense of fearlessness in me that has lasted me through my half-century life so far. Now she panics at the thought of me heading off on my own to some exotic third-world country to do mission work or climb a mountain or jump out of planes and wonders how I'm not afraid. Whenever she brings up my bravery (or brashness, in her opinion), all I can do is thank her.

I consider my case to be an example of good fortune. Things are usually quite the opposite. We often inherit fears through picking up on environmental cues. And now you're going to see exactly how you've been tricked into fear throughout your life.

Once you have identified some of your fears, examine where they are coming from and -- most importantly -- whether they're yours or fears you adopted from others.

Same rule as always: answer honestly, answer thoroughly, and don't stop till you feel it's all down on paper.

What does fear mean to me?

From my perspective, the difference between fear and danger is:

Are my fears rational or irrational?

Consider the source of your fears. Are they based on fact or fiction? Are you simply making up the fearful scenario of what might go wrong or is the fear based on valid information you have gathered? Our minds are rationalization machines, and they're adept at coming up with convincing excuses on the fly.

Is the fear necessary or unnecessary?

We're usually avoiding things, whether through procrastination or denial. Whether it's a real conflict or a potential one, we treat them the same. We feel fear expecting the worst before we've even experienced an outcome.

What you fear must be faced sooner or later. The sooner you take it down, the better. The earlier you face it the more likely you'll have those positive results you may not have expected.

Am I satisfied with the status quo?

Would you be willing to avoid facing your fears even if that means an inability to achieve your dreams? Is the potential outcome of your fear catastrophic (and likely) enough to warrant not even trying?

Transformation Exercise 3:5

Mind Your Perspective

We were to spend 7 days on Mt. Kilimanjaro, working our way up to the peak. This climb was part of a mission trip where we'd committed to climb Kili to raise funds to help Maasai children. The day before, we were given an orientation briefing by our guides. Our lead guide, Ruta, told us that our success on the climb was based on one simple formula – 10% aptitude and 90% attitude.

We were asked to enjoy our difficulties as much as our triumphs. Those difficulties were inevitable on a climb like Kili. If we committed to enjoy our difficulties from the beginning, we'd have a much better time on the climb.

It sounded like simple practical advice to prevent us from giving up, but the lesson was a bit more applicable in life as a whole: mind your perspective and you can do just about anything.

Let's explore.

"You can choose to see a rose bush full of thorns or a thorn bush full of roses." - Abraham Lincoln

How does this statement resonate with you?

"Everything we hear is an opinion not a fact. Everything we see is perspective, not truth." – Marcus Aurelis

Do you believe this statement is true? If not, why? If so, why?

_____

_____

_____

_____

_____

_____

_____

_____

_____

_____

"Your beliefs become your thoughts, your thoughts become your words, your words become your actions, your actions become your habits, your habits become your values, your values become your destiny." - Gandhi

Elaborate on how you can relate to this statement from Gandhi:

_____

_____

_____

_____

_____

_____

"A person is what he or she thinks about all day long." – Ralph Waldo Emerson

What do you think about all day long?

_____

_____

_____

_____

_____

_____

_____

_____

Are you a glass half full or glass half empty type of person?

_____

_____

_____

_____

_____

"Your imagination is your preview of life's coming attractions."

– Albert Einstein

How active is your imagination?

_____

_____

_____
_____
_____

"Every single second is an opportunity to change your life, because in any moment you can change the way you feel." - Rhonda Byrne

Have you ever put this into practice? If so, how?

_____
_____
_____
_____
_____
_____

"Whether you think you can or think you can't, either way you are right."   - Henry Ford

Believing this, how have you put this into practice to your benefit?

_____
_____
_____
_____
_____

Transformation Exercise 3:6

Let's Recap

All the exercises in this Module most likely revealed important truths about the self-imposed fears that limit you.

Make a list of the top ten realizations or any potential awareness that may have been unearthed by these exercises.

1

2

3

4

5

6

7

8

9

10

MODULE 4 – DESIGN YOUR LIFE

In this module we will be fleshing out the foundation you've developed in the previous 3 modules.

The first three exercises are going to draw from the last three; you'll be using discoveries from each to start making specific plans. If some of the questions seem redundant or like you've answered them before (or very similar versions of them) please answer them anyway. Your answers will have changed and become more specific. Trust this process and go with the flow.

We all have goals, and if you're anything like most people I coach (or like me), you have lists and lists smattered across journals and planners that you may have started 5, 10, or 20 years ago.

I've personally run into old journals and notes I've made with lists of goals from decades ago. It comes as no shock that some of the goals look familiar. Those are the goals that have always been true to who I am. They have withstood the test of time and have remained in list after list, year after year.

Does this sound familiar? Who we are at the time that we write our goals or journal entries is a circumstantial being. That's a version of ourselves who was being guided by the times. That's healthy -- it's how we adapt to changes. But you'll often find that some aspirations and character-traits stick around year after year.

Even if you haven't completed a single one of these goals, there's no reason to criticize these lists. On the contrary, you should celebrate the fact that you're a goal-setter, someone willing to put down on paper what others would ignore or deny.

During this module, you'll explore why many of those goals are never checked off the list. Is it a lack of focus? Is it a lack of passion? Is it a lack of vision? Is it a lack of planning? Most likely, the answer to all of those is yes.

Now let's work toward putting those goals in focus.

Transformation Exercise 4:1

Why the need for Self-Discovery?

How do you feel it helped you to start with Self-Discovery?

_____

_____

_____

_____

_____

If you had to pin down three (3) top revelations you found out about yourself during that process, what would they be?

1 _____

2 _____

3 _____

What is your core?

_____

_____

_____

_____

_____

**What important strengths did you discover
that you were not consciously aware of before?**

**Of all that you uncovered during your
self-discovery process, what was your favorite?**

Of all that you uncovered, what surprised you the most?

The Quest for Passion

Why was it so important to dig deep to uncover your passions, especially when it might have been particularly hard to find or admit them to yourself? Because when you're in line with what you desire, the obstacles you'll eventually face don't have as much power against you. You'll start to see them as goalposts instead of brick walls. Also, success doesn't come without passion. And I'm not talking about monetary success I'm talking about the kind of success that fills your heart.

Do you see yourself as a miracle? How?

_____

_____

_____

_____

**What was most surprising regarding the
exploration questions about your passions?**

_____

_____

_____

_____

**List some of the favorite passions you discovered
that you may not have been consciously aware of.**

_____
_____
_____
_____
_____

What surprised you the most about your narrative at the end of Module 2?

_____
_____
_____
_____
_____

Was there anything that didn't make your Top 7, 5 or 3 list during your Quest for Purpose exercise that surprised you?

_____
_____
_____
_____
_____
_____
_____
_____

What *did* make the list that was surprising?

Transformation Exercise 4:3

Importance of your Thoughts

Why was it important to get to the bottom of your thoughts and your limiting beliefs? Because you and I both know that there is no such thing as a straight path. There will always be a challenge, and adversity is a good thing. The very act of overcoming your limiting beliefs will turn you into a person worthy of achieving your goals.

What was revealed during the exercises you did around your thoughts that surprised you?

_____

_____

_____

_____

_____

What limiting beliefs did you have you were not aware of?

_____

_____

_____

_____

_____

How did it feel to discover where some of these came from?

_____

_____

_____

_____

_____

**What were some of your greatest fears
unearthed during the exercise?**

_____

_____

_____

_____

_____

**Were you able to make any connections between the limiting beliefs,
fears and thoughts you discovered are holding you back today from
achieving the life you desire and deserve?**

_____

_____

_____

_____

_____

_____

Transformation exercise 4:4

Overcoming Limiting Beliefs

Just as important as identifying the limiting beliefs that weigh you down is finding ways to overcome them. While there are countless books on the subject, let's take a simple approach that's built on your strengths and helps you focus on how you can change things.

Keep in mind that some beliefs run very deep. In the previous module, you were asked to dig pretty deep to find the cause of these beliefs. Now it's time to do something about them. This 4-step exercise is simple, but powerful, and can be used on every one of your "I can't" or "I'll never" beliefs.

State what hardship is tied to this limiting belief:

_____

_____

_____

_____

_____

State what the actual limiting belief is:

_____

_____

_____

_____

In list form, state what the actual consequences are of holding on to this limiting belief (what are you not accomplishing or achieving because of this belief):

1

2

3

4

5

What challenge or argument do you have for this belief? How can you dispel this limiting belief?

Use some of the strengths and accomplishments you came up with in previous exercises to address this if need be. Remember - you are a miracle!

If necessary, go through this exercise which each of the limiting beliefs you find are hard to let go of. Do each step one by one with each belief until you've disproven the validity of each one. If you work hard enough, you'll find that every argument you make has a counter argument in favor of your success.

Transformation Exercise 4:5

Overcoming Fears

We've established that fear is the opposite of faith. We would all agree that faith and gratitude go hand in hand. One of the greatest paths to overcoming fear is by way of gratitude.

If there is a fear that you find is still standing in your way of accomplishing all that you are meant to accomplish, as with the previous exercise, I want you to do the following for each fear that may have survived your list up to this point.

Exercise Gratitude

In any situation that is instilling or playing on your fear, there is an opportunity to be grateful for something that is a by-product of what you fear. Make a list of what that is before you have to face what you fear.

Set a Goal

For that situation, set a goal that is greater than the fear. List at least one thing you wish to accomplish when you are facing that fear and concentrate on that. Before you know it, your focus will shift from what you fear to your goal.

Divide the Task

Sometimes what we fear is the 'big' picture of something we are trying to accomplish. If you are able to break it down into smaller bite-sized tasks, you'll find that something that at once seemed overbearing and fear-inducing, isn't as severe as originally perceived.

Try Something New

Trying new things tends to stretch and strengthen your courage and bravery muscles. I'm a firm believer in the "Do something every day that scares you" mentality. We're going to get into your Comfort Zone later on but for now, if you HAD to try something new, what would it be?

_____

_____

_____

_____

_____

_____

_____

_____

_____

_____

Ask for Support from Friends and Family

Sharing your fears takes away a lot of what makes them fears. Knowing that there is someone in your corner who believes in you will help your fears lessen quickly. Who can you rely on if you needed to talk through any fears with?

_____

_____

_____

_____

Transformation Exercise 4:6

Your Centenarian Speech

I hope you're ready for some fun. You're now going to write your Centenarian Speech.

Picture you are celebrating your 100th birthday. Someone very close to you will be delivering a speech during the celebration about your life, your accomplishments and your awesomeness.

This person is not modest about you and they are familiar with all of your successes and triumphs. They've covered everything that makes you great. Don't leave anything out – write it all. Written out, the speech has to fill ALL of the lines provided (or more if you'd like to write it elsewhere). Ready? GO!

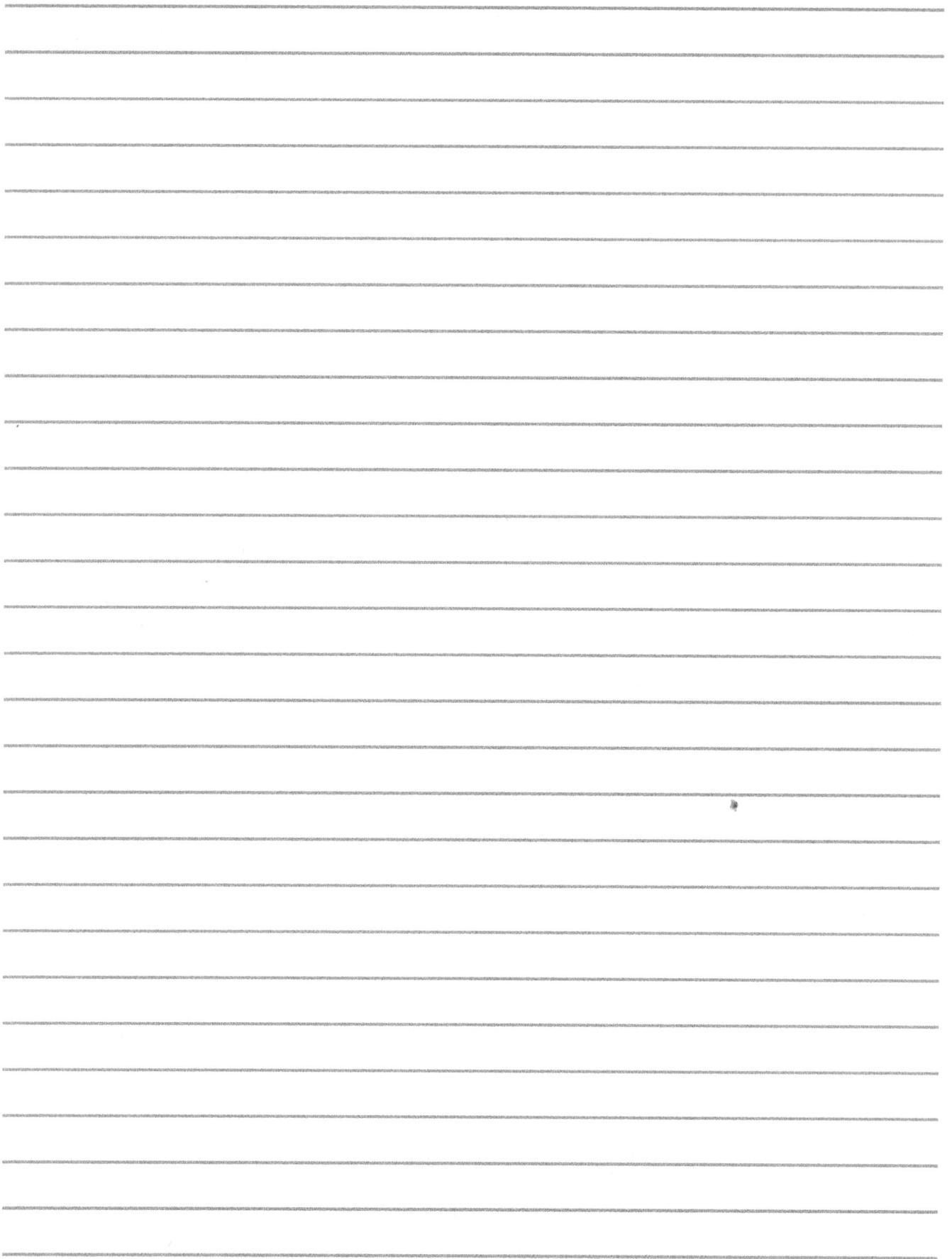

MODULE 5 – DARE TO LIVE IT

As you heard, in this module you are going to actually start setting your goals – the goals that will get you to where you are living your life full of passion, full of what you desire, full of what you deserve – full of YOU!

Working hard to reach your goals and dreams can suck big time when you're in the thick of it. However, when you're doing it in passion and nearing your desired destination, it's one of the most exhilarating feelings you can experience.

That's the reason you've taken the time before this module to set the foundation to discover and uncover your passions – you'll find yourself achieving your goals with tremendous ease when you are operating from a place of following your passion and your purpose.

For this module, ask yourself – "What goals should I be working toward?"

Transformation Exercise 5:1

Let's Explore the Comfort Zone

I personally define a comfort zone *as a graveyard of potential and hope*. That's the gist of it, at least. There's a whole lot more nuance to it than that, but understanding toxic comfort *it is absolutely* where all dreams go to die. It is where lack, mediocrity and low expectations thrive. No life worth living can be lived within the confines of a comfort zone.

"Life begins at the end of your comfort zone." – Neale Donald Walsh

What does this statement mean to you?

_____

_____

_____

_____

_____

Based on my definition of a comfort zone,
do you feel you may be in a bit of a comfort zone right now?

_____

_____

_____

_____

_____

What is so 'comfortable' about your zone right now?
How comfortable is it really?

Sometimes our comfort zones can be the most uncomfortable places we can find ourselves in but fear keeps us there.

What fears are keeping you stuck in your comfort zone today?

Transformation Exercise 5:2

Comfort Zone vs Limiting Beliefs

Do you feel there may be any overlaps between your comfort zone and any of the limiting beliefs you'd addressed earlier in previous modules?

If so, in narrative form, write out what the correlations may be. If you can't find any correlation, dig a bit more. Go back to your notes if you feel it may be helpful.

Transformation Exercise 5:3

The Re-Write

Remember how you were asked to keep that Centenarian Speech handy?

Since you've explored a bit of your comfort zone and made any necessary correlations between that and your limiting beliefs, let's tweak the speech. Take a moment to close your eyes and actually visualize yourself stepping outside of the boundaries of your comfort zone. Visualize the version of yourself that's free of your limiting beliefs.

Now take the speech you wrote and read it to yourself. Without these limiting beliefs and outside of your comfort zone, is there anything you would add to your speech? Perhaps something you may have left out before you had 'permission' to step outside of your box? Is there anything that would look different? What more would you have done? What more would you have given yourself credit for? What more would you be celebrating?

Again, with no limitations of space – physical, mental or emotional – fine tune your speech. If you feel it was perfect as originally written, you may leave it as is.

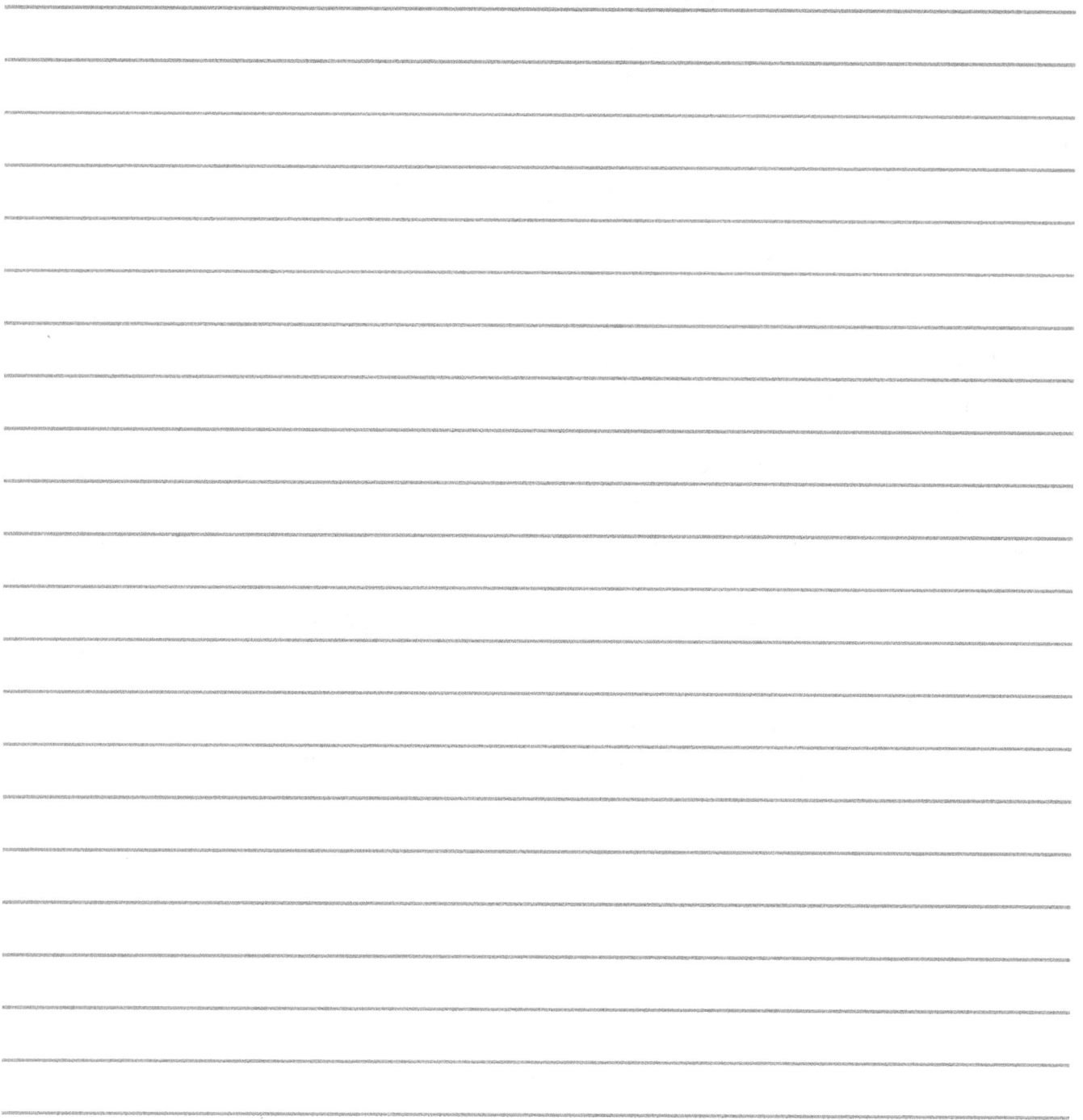

Transformation Exercise 5:4

Goal Setting Primer

Make a new list of long-term goals.

1

2

3

4

5

6

7

8

9

10

Review your list. Do any of these coincide with your Top 7, 5 or 3 from your Quest for Purpose Exercise?

_____

_____

_____

_____

What do these results reveal to you?

_____

_____

_____

_____

How serious are you about accomplishing your goals?

_____

_____

_____

_____

_____

_____

Why do you want your goal?

_____

_____

_____

_____

_____

Why is this goal important to you?

_____

_____

_____

_____

_____

What are the outcomes –
what will come from you achieving your goals?

_____

_____

_____

_____

_____

_____

Imagine your desired outcome.
How will achieving your goals benefit you?

_____

_____

_____

_____

_____

What is most important about your goal? What MUST happen?

_____

_____

_____

_____

Why did you choose these goals?

_____

_____

_____

_____

_____

_____

What would it take for you to achieve these goals right now?

_____

_____

_____

_____

_____

_____

_____

_____

Are these goals only for you? Who else might they benefit?

_____

_____

_____

_____

_____

_____

_____

Transformation Exercise 5:5

Is There Alignment?

Now that you have a new list of goals, compare your list of long-term goals with your centenarian speech. Is there alignment there? In other words, are the goals that you've set for yourself going to help make your speech a reality on your 100th birthday? Imagine that your speech is the "end address" you enter into your GPS and your goals are the directions.

If there are goals missing from your list that are required to design the life you want to live, the one you want reflected by the time you're 100, write those down here:

_____

_____

_____

_____

_____

_____

_____

_____

_____

_____

_____

Are you able to implement these?
What needs to change, the goals or the speech? Explain:

Transformation Exercise 5:6

These are My Goals

All the exercises in this module were designed to help you determine your target. Without that, there's nowhere to aim. Sure, it's difficult to get somewhere without good directions, but it's almost impossible to get somewhere if you have no idea where it is. To achieve, you have to know what you want to achieve.

These are my goals:

_____

_____

_____

_____

_____

_____

_____

_____

_____

_____

_____

MODULE 6 – TAKING ACTION

Welcome to Module 6 and again congratulations of reaching the (arguably) most important stage of your journey: the part where you actually start it.

During this next few module, you will be charting the course to live the life you deserve.

All the work you've done during the previous modules have prepared you for achievement and greatness: you've laid out the groundwork for the abundance to come.

As I mentioned, you've already bridged the gap between who you were and who you know you want to be. You've also bridged the gap between how you were and how you know you need to be.

These were necessary steps before you build that final "bridge." Now you are going to complete your personal transformation by building the bridge between where you are and where you want to be. This is where the magic happens.

Just as a side note (it doesn't have to be right now) you should purchase a journal at some point between now and the last exercise in this Module.

Transformation Exercise 6:1

Your Bridge

Let's explore the bridges you've built so far.

What has changed in "WHO" you are?

_____

_____

_____

_____

_____

_____

_____

_____

What has changed in "HOW" you are?

_____

_____

_____

_____

_____

Describe how your definition of you today varies from that definition of you from Module 1.

_____

_____

_____

_____

_____

_____

_____

_____

_____

_____

_____

_____

How would you say you are better equipped today to take action towards achieving your goals?

Example: Does having a clearer vision of your passion make it easier to take action steps? Did dealing with some limiting beliefs and doubts add energy to your process? Etc.

_____

_____

_____

_____

Transformation Exercise 6:2

Action Plan – Part I

Make a mind-map of the Plan of Action you feel you must take now, in general.

Is there alignment between this, your list of goals and centenarian speech from module 5?

_____

_____

_____

_____

_____

If your goals are not aligned, which one resonates most with you today? Why?

_____

_____

_____

_____

_____

_____

_____

_____

Go back to your plan of action list. Did you set dates or deadlines for each plan? If not, go back and do so now.

_____

_____

_____

_____

_____

_____

_____

_____

How did it feel to have to put dates to everything – to have a deadline?

Uncomfortable? Comfortable? Exciting? Nerve-racking?

_____

_____

_____

_____

_____

_____

Action Plan – Part III

Make a list based on your mind-map (or anything else you come up with) in chronological order (the closest deadline first, the furthest last). List the actions you need to take to begin achieving the goals you've set for yourself.

How'd it feel to put things down in a chronological order?
Did it make it feel more achievable?

Does it bring a new sense of urgency with it?

Transformation Exercise 6:3

Your Pyramid of Success

The main purpose of these Action Plans was to provide a bit of clarity on what comes next.

From what you've developed here, you should be able to identify your pyramid. Your pyramid will provide a good visual reference point as to what you may need to tackle first, so that you can build to your next steps, and then the next and so on.

Let's use a little imagination and visualization. I want you to imagine that you have a perfectly fertile, wonderfully lush garden which is your soul.

Till the Soil: The first thing you need to do is till the soil. This is actually what you have been doing during the last 5 Modules. You have been preparing the soil to make it as fertile and fruitful for all the greatness and abundance you have coming to you.

If there is anything you need to address or feel you haven't really completed in the previous exercises, this is the time to complete those. Give yourself a date by when this task will be completed. My recommendation: don't delay this more than a couple of days. You've done a lot of great work through now, trust that you are open to receiving all the goodness. If tweaking is needed however, tweak now.

Till the Soil

Goal _____ Date: _____

Goal _____ Date: _____

Anything come up?

Plant the Seeds: Then you are going to plant the seeds. These seeds are the dreams, accomplishments and all that you want to come to fruition; they are what you will reap when you are living your best life – when you become the best version of yourself. What you will have and who you will be on the other side of your bridge.

Plant the Seeds

Goal _____ Date: _____
Goal _____ Date: _____

List all your seeds here. This list will include many of what you have explored throughout your journey however, from this list you will come up with your top two. The chances are these top two will be in direct correlation with your truest passions. All the others that don't make it to your top two you will find are very likely subcategories of one or the other. Try it. This will be a fun exercise.

_____

_____

_____

_____

_____

_____

_____

_____

_____

_____

_____

_____

_____

Water the Soil: This is an important part of the process. Just as seedlings that are planted in the ground, your 'seeds' should never dry out, so water them as often as you can while they are in this newly planted stage. What's the best way to keep them properly watered – focus on your vision!

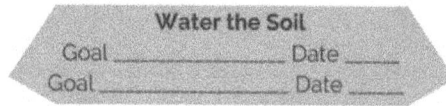

Water the Soil
Goal _____ Date _____
Goal _____ Date _____

I've been looking forward to this portion for some time. It's time to introduce you (or re-introduce you) to Vision Boards. To put it as simply as possible, creating a space for yourself which displays what you want ACTUALLY does bring it to life. It really is that simple(ish). You see, what we focus on becomes our reality.

Creating a Vision Board will give you clarity and will help reinforce your attention on your intentions for your life. Placing it where you see it every day, several times subconsciously activates powerful visualization-to-reality exercises without deliberately trying. If what you put on that board is what you truly love, it will inspire you every time it's in your scope of vision.

Visualization is one of the most powerful mind exercises we can do. Your Vision Board should focus on HOW you want to feel, not just on those things that you want to attain. How you want to feel in your life is as important, if not more so than what you actually want.

In a nutshell, a Vision Board should display images that are representative of who you want to be in your life, of all that you want to do in your life as well as all that you want to have in your life.

Your mind responds very strongly to visual stimulation. Since you are representing your goals, dreams and desires with pictures, images and words, you are actually stimulating your emotions and changing your mindset about your behaviors. What you visualize, you will approach. Visualization and maintaining your focus on what you desire, will drive your actions, will guide your steps and will fuel the work you will be putting into place to achieve your desired outcome.

Before you go on, I want you to take some time to build your vision board. You can use a poster board of whatever size you choose, big enough to hold a good number of pictures but small enough that you can display it prominently in a space you pass by quickly. You know where it's not so big that you will feel tempted to roll it up with a rubber band and toss it in your closet. You have to be able to see it, every day, several times a day. A bathroom is a great place, in front of your toilet is even better.

Once you're completed your board, BELIEVE IT IS ALREADY YOURS!!

By the way, your vision board represents your dreams, your goals and your ideal life. In other words - your vision board, your rules. Remember, there are no rules.

In addition to your vision board, **what else can you do to 'keep your soul well-watered'?** What other ideas can you explore that would help you maintain your focus on your dreams and goals? We'll give you a few examples down the line in this module, but for now, feel encouraged to come up with an idea or two of your own.

_____

_____

_____

_____

_____

_____

_____

_____

Mulch your Garden: When planting an actual garden, gardeners use mulch to help keep weeds out and water in. In other words, the mulch protects the soil, seeds and eventually the growing plants by keeping the bad out and letting the good in. It's the same way with your soul garden. The way to keep the 'water' in is with maintaining your focus on your dreams, as with the vision boards.

Mulch your Garden
Goal _____ Date _____
Goal _____ Date _____

The way you keep the 'weeds' out is to mind your tribe! How would you describe your tribe?

_____

_____

_____

_____

_____

_____

_____

_____

_____

_____

_____

_____

_____

_____

This concept of you really being as good as the company you keep is as old as time. Proverbs 13:20 says "Go with wise men and be wise: but he who keeps company with the foolish will be broken.

If the people we associate with is so critical to our success, why do most of us select people at the same level of success?

_____

_____

_____

_____

_____

_____

_____

**How do other people's beliefs,
habits and philosophies become our own?**

_____

_____

_____

_____

_____

_____

_____

_____

_____

_____

_____

If you isolated yourself from average thinkers more often, would you be more successful?

_____

_____

_____

_____

_____

_____

_____

_____

_____

_____

This is a crucial concept and one that deserves careful attention. You will get into the concept of Masterminds in an upcoming Module and I encourage you to experience the power of that process.

It is important for you to see how you feel about this for now but know that you will be digging much deeper into this concept of tribe further down the road.

These previous few exercises should help you complete your Pyramid of Success the purpose of which is to establish a visual concept of what your next steps will look like. Complete this and include dates for everything.

YOUniversal Success Pyramid ©

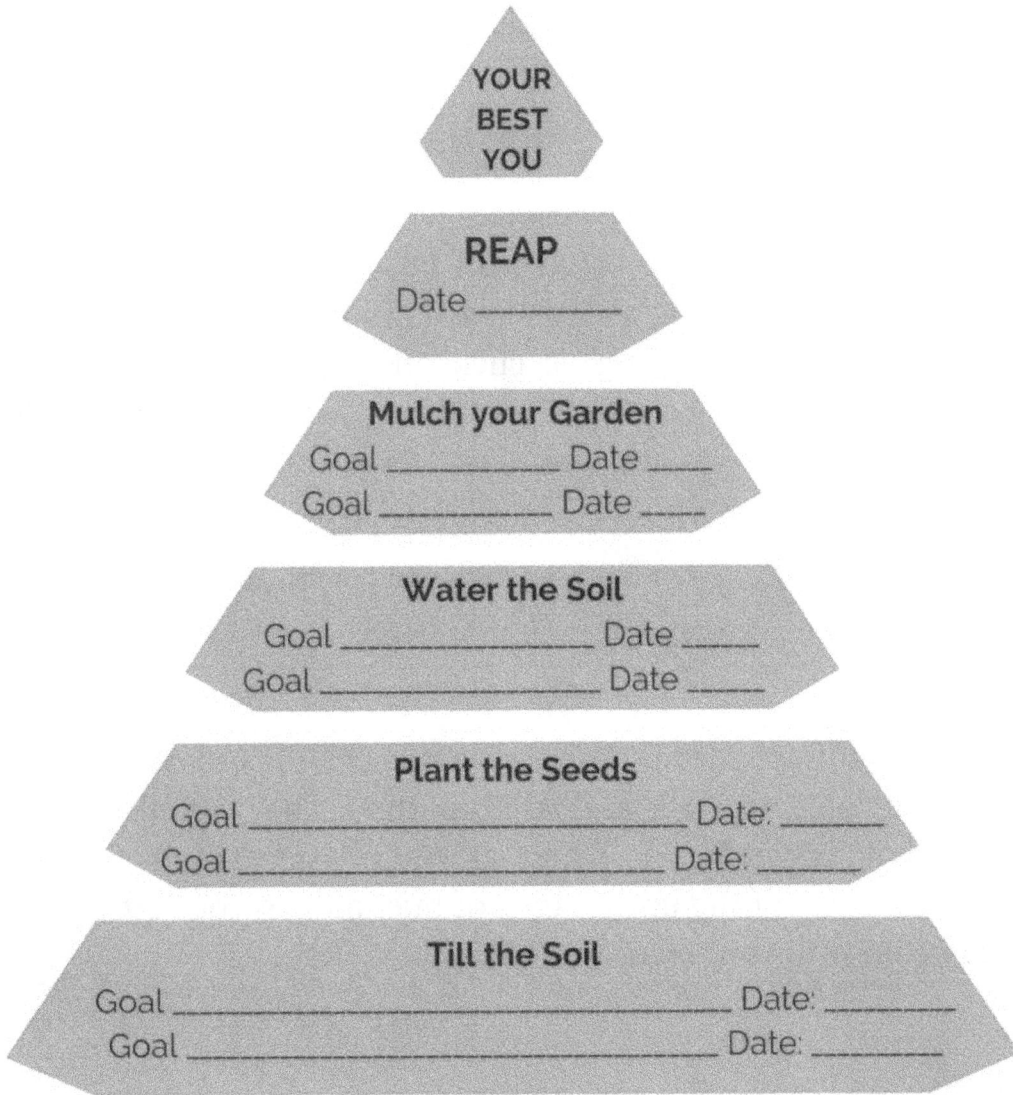

YOUR
BEST
YOU

REAP
Date _____

Mulch your Garden
Goal _____ Date _____
Goal _____ Date _____

Water the Soil
Goal _____ Date _____
Goal _____ Date _____

Plant the Seeds
Goal _____ Date: _____
Goal _____ Date: _____

Till the Soil
Goal _____ Date: _____
Goal _____ Date: _____

Transformation Exercise 6:4

Managing Your Time

What is the most effective way to sabotage your goals?

Procrastination.

Procrastination is nothing more than the art of trying to keep up with all you didn't do yesterday.

We've become a society obsessed with busyness. And I'm not talking about the productive kind. I'm talking about always doing something whether it's good for us or not. Whether we're falling for clickbait on Facebook or surfing YouTube for something to cure our boredom, we flit around from distracting task to distracting task. When we procrastinate, whatever we look for is never the thing that actually demands our attention.

Why do we procrastinate? Because it's easier. Because we get to avoid the task at hand (which we assume will be harder and less rewarding than what we're doing).

Let's start building better time-management habits today. These two "tricks" will help you focus on your goals and what matters. They will almost immediately change the way you live and work. These are simply suggestions, but will help you begin thinking in terms of the importance of maximizing your efficiency. You will eventually come up with your own system.

Technique 1: Plan your day first thing in the morning.

You often don't do what you should be doing because you're bombarded every day with a thousand fires to put out. When you don't have anything written down, they're just ideas swimming around in your head. It's almost impossible to pick out the right ones at the right times. That's why you're going to start writing things down.

As early in the day as is feasible, sit at your desk (or your bed or your meditation mat) for ten minutes and write down what needs to be done during the day.

Think of the important things first based on your most productive priorities and then bring it down to the more "you-centric" things like personal hobbies. You're not going to set times or anything of the sort. You're just making a "check-list" that you can bring with you to make sure you've done everything that needs to be done.

Fit in everything you'd like to do. Don't be shy. If there's something totally personal on there that seems ridiculous to add (because you think you don't have enough time) keep it in.

When you prioritize and plan ahead of time, you'll find you have plenty of time to do the things that you want to do after you've done what's necessary.

Once you get into the swing of check-listing things, you can then start to block time for it. Don't be too frugal with your hours. Use up as much of your day as you can. Hobbies also count in this time so, if you like to read, set a fair amount of time to read and unwind.

Some people don't like the time-scheduling aspect, and that's fine. If simply keeping a checklist works better for you, do it that way, for now anyway. But do use one of the systems. You will see some amazing changes within the next week if you stick to it.

Technique 2: Blocking

Some people call it the Pomodoro technique, others call it intervals. Blocking is a way to micro-manage tasks and increase your efficiency (thus freeing up more time for your passions).

How does it work?

By setting interval times (such as the popular 25/5) you give yourself an intensive work period followed by a quick "break" period in between. This allows you to prevent work burnout while guaranteeing that you're using every minute to the highest potential.

In this day and age there are a plethora of options when it comes to apps that will help you time block for increased efficiency. In that block of work time, you must be stalwart in keeping out distractions like social media, online videos, email, and even snacking. Focus on one task and only that task.

Then, when your break times come up (usually 5 to 15 minutes), you cannot work. This allows you to take a legitimate moment to yourself to recoup and enjoy a wind-down before getting back into work.

This technique can actually cut your work time in half, as it prevents you from spinning out on a procrastination journey in between the tougher work. That means you'll get the hard work done faster and have more time to do the things you love to do (like your hobbies). Seriously, try it.

This all starts out with respect for your time. When you respect how many hours you have in a day – and are disciplined about using them – you'll find a better life comes naturally from it.

Remember, "The harder you push yourself, the harder your 'self' pushes back." – Anonymous.

Where do you believe you can improve as far as your time management is concerned? How would this improvement help in achieving the goals you've laid out for yourself?

Transformation Exercise 6:5

Get Out of Your Own Way!

Since you've undoubtedly revealed and proven to yourself how amazing you are and how deserving you are of achieving all that you are destined to achieve, you will believe when someone says you have within you the potential to accomplish anything you set your mind and heart to. With that said, please take a moment to look at yourself in the mirror. You see that person looking back, that's your only competition. That's it.

Everything that you desire is something you want, right?

Right.

So all you have to do is get out of your own way and reach out for it. Everything you are passionate about and everything that you dream of is yours already. All you have to do is reach out and get it.

Let's explore how best to do this.

Let it fly.

If you look hard enough, you will undoubtedly find a reason why you shouldn't do something or other. When this thought creeps up, just let it fly! Push yourself through any insecurity that may be standing in your way. You'll find that once you begin so too will the momentum set in motion your ability to overcome any obstacles or barriers trying to stand in your way.

How will you 'let it fly'?

Take it Step by Step.

When we have things we need to get done, particularly after all the excitement you've built up during this process, surely you're ready to get going. Resist the urge to do everything at once. You are more productive when you focus your attention on doing one task at a time, then the next, and then the next. The accomplishing of these tasks will stack up quickly, don't worry.

How will you pace yourself to take things step by step?

_____

_____

_____

_____

_____

Consistency is the name of the game.

Being consistent will help you not only maintain your focus but will help you reach success in a fraction of the time. Focus on keeping your eye on the prize.

Aristotle said, "We are what we repeatedly do. Excellence, then, is not an act, but a habit."

What does this mean to you?

_____

_____

_____

_____

_____

Consider your Impact

Without a doubt, your success is going to influence more than just yourself. Not only on a tangible level, but your success has the potential to ignite passion in others that will ultimately lead them to succeed and that sequence will continue. Your motivation will motivate others; your success will inspire others to succeed.

Consider the potential impact you will have on those around you and ultimately the world.

What excites you the most about your ability to change the world in a positive way?

Transformation Exercise 6:6

The New You

You've done so much great work. I'm proud of you for investing your time and effort to achieve astronomic success. You really should pat yourself on the back. Many people wouldn't take this to task, considering how difficult it is to be honest with yourself about what you want.

For the final exercise of this Module, you're going to bring together a lot of what you've done to this point. You're going to need that new journal mentioned at the beginning of this Module.

Take your journal and on the first page, you're going to write your title "I Am _____ (your name here)" and the date.

The first thing you're going to write in this journal is a narrative of who you are today, how you are today and where you are today.

Describe what your dreams are and how you will feel once they've all been achieved. Who have you had to become to achieve them? What have you had to change to become that person? Who are you surrounding yourself with? What have you had to let go of? What has been the greatest realization about yourself throughout the process?

I could go on and on but you get the point right? Basically, you are celebrating the fruits of your labor and your time to reap what you have sown. Celebrate – you've earned it!

TAKE ACTION –

HIGH ACHIEVEMENT MODULE I

YOUR TIME

You spent a bit of time during Module 6 learning about tips and ways you can keep yourself from wasting time or procrastinating. Now you'll be taking a good look at your planning/calendar system. Do you use one? If you do, which one do you use?

If you're not currently using one, how many have you tried in the past? Have they worked for you?

Here's a bit of truth about time management planning systems. Truly, ALL of them work and NONE of them work. From the simplest to the most complicated planning systems they all ONLY WORK IF YOU USE THEM!

ACHIEVEMENT TIP #1

A good calendar system will have a place for you to do the following:

a) Write down your long term goals and dreams – preferably 5 years, 3 years, 1 year and 3 months.

b) Break down steps you need to take to achieve each one – with a trackable system so that you can set dates along the way by when you have to achieve each task for the overall goal.

c) Write down what you are celebrating.

d) Draw if you need to mind-map.

e) Recap either weekly or monthly to make sure you are staying on track.

f) Make plenty of notes you can refer to when you are in planning mode.

g) Most importantly, make sure there is space for ACCOUNTABILITY.

These are just ideas of some of what a planning system should include. Believe it or not, there is tremendous power in crossing or checking something off a list. When you make a list of tasks each day and check or cross them off as you achieve them, by the end of the day you will have hard visual evidence of all that you have accomplished. It feels good and you feel productive, and that's important in your journey to accomplishing your goals.

If you are happy with your current system, great – keep using it. As long as you feel it is an effective tool for focus and goal-driven action. If you don't have something you're happy with, find it or create it. By now no doubt you've explored enough systems that you realize what works for you and what doesn't. As mentioned, if you want to fine-tune one to your needs, pick and choose your favorite parts of all the planning systems and create one that encompasses your needs.

ACHIEVEMENT TIP #2

Make sure you are aware of the difference between tasks and goals. Review your list of goals before you start completing your planner or calendar system. Some of the goals you may have listed may actually be tasks you need to complete to achieve a larger goal. Examine them and see what comes up for you.

ACHIEVEMENT TIP #3

Calendar in even your hobbies and things you enjoy doing. Make sure that you are taking the time to celebrate your wins, have some fun, enjoy yourself and relax. This should be happening at a very minimum on a weekly basis. Make space for it in your life and in your calendar.

ACTION PLAN

Your action plan is to choose or create a calendar system that will fit your lifestyle so that you can use it with ease to keep you on track. This is something you will be using daily, reviewing monthly and with a fine-tooth comb, evaluating quarterly.

Now is the time to find an accountability partner as well.

YOUR GOALS

During the previous Modules, you worked on tweaking and narrowing down what your goals are. You've also had time to work on your Success Pyramid. Certainly there was alignment with your list of goals and the steps you are taking to make your way up your Success Pyramid.

Review the dates you entered on your Success Pyramid. How do those goals and dates resonate with you today? Are those goals appropriately positioned to get you where you want to be by when you want to be there? Take some time to review that and make any revisions necessary to make sure that everything you are doing is in alignment with your dream life.

Once you've explored that, take your calendar and fill in that road map. Using what you read above in TIP #1, make sure you are hitting at least the markers described above. If you don't want to go out through the entire year, go out at least as far as 3 months down the line.

Remember: you don't have to know everything you want to plan in those 3 months, but you must establish waypoints in those 3 months so you can stay on task toward meeting your goals.

ACHIEVEMENT TIP #4

At a minimum, you should be able to have a target 3-month goal. From there, you'll be setting monthly, weekly, and daily goals.

ACTION PLAN

Your action plan will be to review your list of goals and your Success Pyramid. You will be reviewing these alongside your calendar system to ensure that everything that you are doing is in alignment with achieving your goals. Along the way, celebrate your successes and reward yourself. Achieving your dreams isn't about suffering through hard work and toiling away. Have fun with it and love what you do while you get where you want to be.

YOUR NETWORK

Webster's defines a Network as a group or system of interconnected people or things.

How do you define your network?

Your network or your circle of influence can be a key component in achieving your goals, particularly those surrounding your business or financial goals. It is said that the average person knows approximately 250 people. Out of that large group, very few may be true friends, but that doesn't mean you can't have meaningful and fruitful relationships with acquaintances, which will oftentimes leads to friendships.

And what if you want to have an above average list of acquaintances? Get out there and get to know more people.

Networking in a nutshell is simply meeting new people, conversing with them, making connections and developing relationships to grow your circle of influence. By developing what will develop into long-term relationships where your main focus is adding value to their lives, you create lasting impressions with people. You are also fine-tuning an important life skill which has many applications for you both professionally and personally.

As you build these relationships, those people receiving value from your relationship will reciprocate that value. Naturally, people benefit people. That's how society is meant to work.

Among the many benefits of networking, consider the following:

In a network of people, you can share pertinent information and will gain from the experience of everyone in the group. You can receive answers to some questions you may have about starting, building or growing your business, for example. Different perspectives bring with them a host of benefits, many of which we wouldn't have otherwise from interacting with our small group of close friends or peers.

You can also make some great connections and take advantage of opportunities that will present themselves. You can take the opportunity to promote your business or your next personal venture within your networking group. Building positive relationships within your expanding circle of influence is a great way to expand your reach and create a great buzz and great "word of mouth."

ACHIEVEMENT TIP #5

Some wonderful opportunities for networking venues may be found by attending Chamber of Commerce events and meetings; working with community groups such as Lyons, Kiwanis and Rotary Clubs; Create your own networking events; Industry related events.

If giving back is a big part of who you are, participating in volunteer events in your community is a great way to meet people who are aligned with you who you can build great mutually beneficial relationships with.

ACTION PLAN

Meet/Network

How are you meeting new people/potential clients/potential referral sources?

_____

_____

_____

_____

_____

_____

When you attend a networking event, truly engage with people.

Ask them good questions to get to know them – who they are and what they're passionate about. Don't make these new interactions all about receiving the benefits of networking. Be a real person and build meaningful relationships. From a place of sincerity, you'll begin cultivating mutually beneficial relationships Ask about their FAMILY, OCCUPATION, RECREATION and their MESSAGE.

ACHIEVEMENT TIP #6

People love to answer a question about how they got started in their business or career. This is a great way to spark a conversation.

ACHIEVEMENT TIP #7

Be a great listener. Focus on them and get to know them. You will have an opportunity throughout your relationship for them to get to know you. Initially, focus on them.

ACHIEVEMENT TIP #8

Before you part with someone you've just met, be sure to ask them how you can know if someone you meet might be a good connection for them. They will tell you the type of people they may want to be connected with.

ACTION PLAN

Follow up and Follow Through are crucial!

What's the point of networking if you are not going to follow up? The future of that newly initiated relationship is going to be based on your follow up and your follow through. Don't promise to contact them and "forget" week after week. If you feel like this person is a good fit for your network (and your life), initiate interactions with them and show them they're worth your time.

Here are a few suggestions:

Send a personalized e-mail that stands out. Chances are they will be receiving several other e-mails from others they met however, if you send something that will stand out, you will make a much better impression.

Send a handwritten note. If you have an address on their business card, mail them a handwritten note. If you have one preprinted which also has your contact information, even better. Despite the digital age we live in, people love receiving cards in the mail.

Send them your blog. When you first send it, send it only on a blog/article you may have written which they may find relevant to peak their interest. Invite them to sign up for your blog however, if they don't sign up, do not continue to send it.

Add value. E-mail articles which they may find interesting or helpful to their line of work or something you may have discussed during your meeting. A note or something which says "Thought you might find this interesting" or "Was thinking of you when I read this" will go a long way to make them feel you were present, paying attention, and interested in what they had to say.

Any of these suggestions go a long way to establish a great foundation for your new relationship.

ACHIEVEMENT TIP #9

Use a service like redstamp.com which allows you to send digital 'Nice to Meet You' card-style e-mails. You have a wide variety of options but using one where you can include your photo will help them place the name to the face. This option makes a big difference because chances are you may run into them again.

ACHIEVEMENT TIP #10

Business Cards: Instead of focusing on being a business card distributor at networking events, dedicate yourself to collecting business cards and engaging with people enough that you remember who they are. If need be, write down a few notes in the back of their business cards (not necessarily right in front of them) with something you can follow up on.

For example: You're speaking with someone who has their daughter's graduation coming up in a couple of days. Write down the graduation date behind the card and on that day, send a brief e-mail congratulating them. Also include something of value with the e-mail if you are able. Personalization makes us feel important and loved, and it can really make someone's day.

ACTION PLAN

Be a connector/resource:

Make great value-based introductions. E-mail mutual introductions are a great way to connect people who may be able to establish a mutually beneficial relationship with each other. Be sure you have asked for permission from both parties as a professional courtesy. Whenever possible, provide them with referrals.

ACTION PLAN

Don't be shy to ask for referrals. Just as you enjoy helping make connections, so will they. Make sure that you make it easy for others to network for you and on your behalf. What's the best way of doing this? By educating them about what you offer.

Create your Benefit Statement:

Make sure you know what this is so that you can easily tell others. Let your potential referral sources know what benefits you offer to your target market. They cannot refer or promote you unless they know what you offer.

What is your Benefit Statement?

_____

_____

_____

_____

_____

_____

_____

_____

If you don't have one readily available, take your time to create one. Head to Google and do some searches on "elevator pitches" and learn to condense your personal mission and talents. This will go a long way in maximizing the potential of your networking efforts.

This will be a great way for your potential referral sources to know when they meet or come in contact with someone who may be a good referral source for you.

YOUR TRIBE

The concept of the "master mind alliance" was introduced by Napoleon Hill in his book from the 1920s, The Law of Success, and expanded upon in his 1930s book, Think and Grow Rich. While Napoleon Hill called it a "master mind alliance," it's been shortened and modernized to "mastermind group." Mastermind groups have been around since the beginning of time.

Mastermind groups offer a combination of brainstorming, education, peer accountability and support in a group setting to sharpen your business and personal skills. A mastermind group helps you and your mastermind group members achieve success. Participants challenge each other to set powerful goals, and more importantly, to accomplish them.

Through a mastermind group process, first you create a goal, then a plan to achieve it. The group helps you with creative ideas and decision-making. Then, as you begin to implement your plan, you bring both success stories and problems to the group.

Success stories are applauded (loudly!), and problems are solved through peer brainstorming and collective, creative thinking. The group requires commitment, confidentiality, willingness to both give and receive advice and ideas, and support each other with total honesty, respect and compassion. Mastermind group members act as catalysts for growth, devil's advocates and supportive colleagues. This is the essence and value of mastermind groups.

ACHIEVEMENT TIP #11

Examine your tribe. Revisit what you discovered in Module 6. Can you determine if there is a common denominator? Look for similarities or a common thread among everyone in your tribe. Evaluate your situation. What needs to change the most or what would you like to change most? Can that be changed if you stay within your tribe? Remember, there is no suggestion of leaving your current tribe altogether.

The only suggestion comes in our need as high achievers to surround ourselves with those who are living and existing in the mindset required to live an exceptional life.

YOUR BRAIN FOOD – YOUR SOUL FOOD

What are you reading? Who are you reading? Why are you reading?

In a world where it has become increasingly important to be conscientiously aware of what we are feeding our bodies, it's curious how people are not equally as aware of what they are feeding their minds and their souls. It's not *as* important, but *more* important. Do you feel that way?

What you are feeding your soul and brain depends on what you are reading, watching and listening to on a daily basis. Think about that. How is what you are absorbing affecting how you are living your life?

Do you see a correlation? If you don't, I guarantee you're not looking hard enough. Do you know people who are negative, all gloom and doom, and can't get "unstuck?" 9/10 times, these people spend a great deal of time listening to the news or subconsciously or consciously surrounding themselves with negative talk. It is impossible to expect that what they are feeding their minds (the inside of their life) will not begin to affect what is going on outside of their life.

ACHIEVEMENT TIP #12

Understandably, people want to be informed. But sometimes we take in too much news and feel dread for all of the things that are happening out there. We worry about things we can't control, and that's unhealthy. There is no need to be constantly glued to your televisions or other platforms constantly watching or reading the news. Try to go on a 'No-News' diet.

Give yourself some time away from the negativity going on out there. There is a lot more positivity out there than you think, it just doesn't pull in as much money as the negative stuff. As for you, as someone who is on a journey to live the best of your life, deliberately stay away from the negative.

ACTION PLAN

READ. READ. READ! As often as you can, read books that will help you prepare and fertilize your mindset. If you don't know where to start, don't worry. Surely you have people you look up to – mentors, teachers or people who are already living a life similar to the life you want. Ask them what they are reading and read that! Ask them what books have influenced them and read those books. Successful people LOVE that question and they will often have plenty of recommendations for you.

ACHIEVEMENT TIP #13

Remember when you were working on your calendar and thinking of how to make time for those things you loved to do? You should have time blocked every day for reading, EVERY DAY! It doesn't matter whether it's 10 minutes or an hour. You need to be reading every day, period.

ACHIEVEMENT TIP #14

Don't like to read? There are people who really find it hard to set aside time to read because, in all honesty, they simply don't like to read. For those of you who fall into this category, don't worry. Get yourself signed up for Audible or other platforms like Hoopla (which offers free audio and e-books through your library) where you can listen to audio books. This will change your life. You can nourish your mind and soul easily while you drive, during your workout or anytime that you can listen to your books.

ACHIEVEMENT TIP #15

Invest in an e-reader. One of the best decisions you can make might be investing in an e-reader. They are easy to transport and when someone recommends a great book you can't wait to get into, all you have to do is download it.

ACHIEVEMENT TIP #16

Don't forget to make good use of your public library. Your library is a great resource for recommendations, books galore and what I love most is that since you can only check books out for a certain amount of time, you have to read them before they are due back.

ACTION PLAN

Choose a book you are going to start reading/listening to today. Do you have that book in mind already? Chances are someone has gifted you a book you've had sitting around collecting dust. Think about who gifted it or recommended it. Schedule it!

STAY FOCUSED –

HIGH ACHIEVEMENT MODULE II

YOUR VISION

When you are truly in alignment with your passions, the obstacles and unpredictable ups-and-downs will never get in your way.

Your mind is immeasurably powerful, so there's no doubt it has an influence on your path in life. The vision you hold for yourself is exactly where your brain leads you. Think negatively and you'll often find yourself in bad situations. Think positively and you'll find constant success.

Have you created your Vision Board? If so, how does it make you feel when you look at it? How often are you looking at it? Did you place it somewhere where you see it (even if only subconsciously because you've grown so accustomed to it) several times per day? Remember, the operative word here is FOCUS.

ACHIEVEMENT TIP #1

If your Vision Board is so small that you keep it in a drawer, go back to the drawing board. If it's too large that you can't see it fitting anywhere, go back to the drawing board. Make sure the size is just right for it to be prominently displayed. My favorite place is in the bathroom (right on a corner of your mirror is hard to ignore) or in front of the desk where you are working most of the day. Make it fit so you can make it work!

ACHIEVEMENT TIP #2

Many people talk about having a dream journal or a dream book (the goal kind of dream, not the sleep kind). That's all fine and dandy, but if it becomes a task instead of an exciting part of your day, it's going to be hard to make it habitual. Make FOCUSING on your dreams as easy for yourself as possible.

ACHIEVEMENT TIP #3

When you are clear and focused on what you want, it will show up in your life. Chances are those things have always been there, you just have a new sense of perspective and focus that lets you see them. The clearer your goals and dreams, the easier you'll be able to see subtle paths to them.

ACTION PLAN A (If you already have your Vision Board)

Review your Vision Board picture by picture, word by word. Take half a minute to focus on each picture and word. How does your body feel? How about your mind? Is it racing with confidence or nervous energy? Let that feeling stick around for a while, even if you're feeling discomfort.

Look toward the future as if you're already there. How do you feel living that life? Who have you become in order to achieve what is on your Vision Board? What have you accomplished to get there? Who is enjoying this journey with you?

ACTION PLAN B (If you don't already have your Vision Board)

Grab your calendar and, within the next week, give yourself a definitive, immovable date to create your vision board. Make sure you plan so that you have all the 'ingredients' you'll need to create it at the time and date that you set for it. Don't sabotage your ability to complete it by not planning. Remember, you deserve this and this is a very powerful tool in living your exceptional life.

In case you don't remember exactly how to make your vision board, below are the directions taken directly from the vision board module.

Your Vision Board should focus on HOW you want to feel, not just on those things that you want to attain. How you want to feel in your life is as important, if not more so than what you actually want.

In a nutshell, a Vision Board should display images that are representative of who you want to be in your life, of all that you want to do in your life as well as all that you want to have in your life.

Our minds respond very strongly to visual stimulation. Since you are representing your goals, dreams and desires with pictures, images and words, you are actually stimulating your emotions, which are the vibrational energy which trigger the law of attraction. What you visualize, you will attract.

YOUR HABITS

Habits can be your greatest ally or your worst enemy. The beautiful thing is that you decide. People often say that bad habits are hard to break. They're right. But guess what? Good habits are just as hard to break. A habit is a habit (is a habit).

Once you slip into the rhythm of practicing good, successful habits, they will be just as hard to break as the bad. It's simply a matter of deciding when to start creating the good practices that will become your good habits.

TIP – you decided to journey into your great practices when you began this program. The good habits you are forming are your key to success.

We've often heard how doing something for 21 days makes it a habit. Have you tried it for yourself? Has it worked? For most people, that 21 day rule doesn't apply. There is no set time in which we build sustainable habits.

Everyone is different, and in order to break bad habits and create successful habits, you must start to create them – plain and simple. Your motivation will get you started but it is the habits that you form that will keep you going.

Action keeps attention engaged. Make sure it's not just busy action but deliberate on-your-path-to-greatness action.

One of the best ways to form a habit is to:

• Determine what you want

• Do an action every day that leads you to what you want.

Forming good habits begins with dreaming big. Having said that, the habits that you create and follow every day are what are going to get you to achieve those dreams.

Let's examine this. You have your dreams which are the goals you want to achieve for yourself. You understand that in order to get there, you must form the habits that will help you become the person you need to be to achieve your dreams. What would those habits be? Only you can determine what those are, but here are a few examples to get you started.

ACHIEVEMENT TIP #4

Let's say you dream about writing a book (a common but often forgotten dream). At first, it may seem daunting. Even if you know what you want to say and know what value your book can bring to readers, getting started seems impossible. You decide to allocate a certain number of words you want to get down each day.

For example, you're going to write 500, 1000 or 1,500 words per day. Before you know it, your book is complete, simply by forming that habit. Setting this allocation for your overall goal makes it easier to see the forest for the trees.

How do you eat an elephant? One bite at a time! (Note: I love elephants. Do not eat elephants.)

ACTION PLAN

Review your goals, passions and dreams list. Review your calendar. What tasks do you have on the path to accomplishing your overall goal?

While you're examining the tasks, start considering smaller habits you can use to finish those tasks. This whole process is about "chunking" the big and scary tasks until you've got no-excuse actions to go through every day.

Start working on those habits today. Set accountability perimeters for yourself or with an accountability buddy. This will go a long way to help you stay on track and, before you know it, your habit is formed.

Remember what Aristotle said: "We are what we repeatedly do. Excellence then is not an act but a habit."

YOUR GENEROSITY

Our society has somewhat programmed us to become consumed with ourselves. The truth is that the road to getting everything and anything you desire is paved with putting others ahead of what you want and focusing on their wants, needs and desires and helping them to fulfill them.

Giving something makes us far happier than receiving something. Even the most selfish people still get an indescribable joy from giving to others. Giving and helping others is part of the divine plan. We are put here on earth to serve. Giving to others is giving to yourself; helping others is helping yourself; Loving others is loving yourself.

If I wanted to make this section immeasurably longer, I'd share hundreds of pages of research that links giving (and service to others) to better health, happiness and even longevity. But we don't even need the science to back it up. Giving is good for the soul, and it's something you can feel. When you give, it's a gift for your own heart.

How are you giving? Where are you giving and to whom? The giving referred to here is not necessarily limited to monetary charity. This giving includes your time and gifts as well. Money makes the world go round, but human interaction sets the soul ablaze.

Think about the last time you served others or witnessed the act of giving. How did that make you feel? Very often, the best way to add fuel to our passions and dreams is to go out and serve others, even if only for a few hours a week.

The best way to receive what you want is to give it away. Your life is like a mirror and whatever you do or give you will receive. It really is that simple.

ACTION PLAN

Look up organizations or local volunteer opportunities in your town. Find something coming up within the next couple of weeks that is helping a cause that resonates with you – something you feel passion for. Sign up to volunteer. If you can find a friend to come with you, great, but that's not necessary.

In fact, chances are you will meet amazing people participating in volunteer activities so go it alone if you must. After the event or activity, journal about how it made you feel. Without a doubt, you'll be looking forward to doing it again.

YOUR GRATITUDE

Do you believe that it is not that happy people are thankful but rather that thankful people are happy? Think about that.

Whether someone sees a cup as half empty or half full has everything to do with how much GRATITUDE they have in their hearts. Your level of gratitude will play the biggest role in determining how you see your life. It will frame your contentment and breathe new life into every moment, no matter how difficult.

Are you being grateful every day? Are you feeling gratitude by default or do you find yourself feeling grateful only when something really big happens? Do your daily "thank you's" come from the heart or are they born of mindless habits?

ACHIEVEMENT TIP #5

Imagine then, if you began to truly show gratitude or appreciation for all those things in your life which are going right and working in your favor, many of which we tend to take for granted. What do you feel can happen to that when you start showing true appreciation for it? Based on what you've just read, it will increase. Try gratitude every day.

Try it for the things you just received and the things you forgot you have. Your health? Your family? Your job? Every single good in your life deserves your appreciation every once-in-a-while. See what happens when you focus on your gratitude for these things daily.

ACHIEVEMENT TIP #6

Let's take it a step further. What if you began to show appreciation and gratitude for what's to come? Think about it. In part of your action plan for gratitude, what would happen if you began to feel and show gratitude for what you want?

For example: You are working on one of your goals and know you have set a completion date for that goal. Begin to show appreciation and gratitude for that goal already having been achieved or accomplished. Begin to, out loud and as if it was already here, thank your higher power for the manifestation of you already having accomplished your goal. How does that feel for you? Perhaps it will feel weird at first.

That's okay, that's even normal in fact. Try it with something small at first. Once it manifests and you've proven to yourself how much power gratitude really has, it will begin to feel more natural.

ACTION PLAN

Begin a Gratitude Journal. Reward yourself with a brand new, nothing else is written inside, journal which you will keep next to where you sleep. Every evening before you go to sleep, take 5 minutes to review your day. Write down a minimum of 5 things that you are grateful for that happened throughout your day.

This will be a great way to hit your pillow in a positive frame of mind but will also ensure that the last thing you do before you settle down for your slumber of dreams is NOT watch the evening news.

When you first wake up, give yourself 5 minutes to fiddle with your journal. If that means you set the alarm clock for 5 minutes before your regularly scheduled time or bypass that 5th snooze, gift yourself these 5 minutes.

In the morning round, you are going to write down a minimum of 5 things that you are grateful WILL HAPPEN throughout your day (remember, as if they are already so). As previously mentioned, this may feel awkward at first, but trust in the process.

There's no need to compare to see if your list from the morning has any overlaps with your list from that evening however, you are almost guaranteed that after several days or weeks of doing these, you will begin to see the correlation.

Subconsciously you will begin to LIVE in a spirit of gratitude. Living in gratitude is going to change EVERYTHING for you in a very positive way – WATCH!

YOUR SELF-TALK

What do you say when you talk to yourself? You covered this a bit during the previous modules, but let's dig deeper. Are you more aware of what you say when you talk to yourself? Are you more aware of what you say when you talk about yourself?

When you introduce a new idea into the brain, there's going to be cognitive dissonance at first. It may feel uncomfortable. The brain doesn't necessarily like new ideas, especially if they conflict with older beliefs that you've embraced in the past. So, if you spent years nurturing low self-esteem and you suddenly decide to introduce the notion that you are truly a wonderful person, two unreal circuits must compete. The old memory and the new idea.

When something new comes in, the brain goes into an alert state. The amygdala is saying "wake up, pay attention, there's something different happening in my body or the world. Is it safe or dangerous?"

You need to hang tight through this period of discomfort as you realign your life with your passions.

When you focus on the big questions, the really big questions, you are challenging your brain to think outside the box, and this causes the structure of our neurons to change. Our frontal lobe (the part that controls logic, reason, language, consciousness and compassion) is especially responsive.

New axons grow, reaching out to new dendrites to communicate in new ways your brain has never experienced. When contemplating the big questions, you use your frontal lobe to alter the function of the other parts of the brain. Don't be afraid to THINK BIG!

ACHIEVEMENT TIP #7

Once you begin your journey with dedication and purpose, please focus on what you do right, celebrate your wins, focusing on the things you do well. This will help you improve and hone your skills more effectively. Merely focus on fixing whatever is going wrong can keep you in a negative mindset. But when you focus on improving what's going right, you bring along more positive change.

ACHIEVEMENT TIP #8

Accept the fact that you are allowed (and deserve) to live an extraordinary life! Decide today, right now, that you are going to choose what you really want from life and then you're going to figure out how to get it.

ACTION PLAN

Write down your affirmations/declarations on index cards, a journal that you carry with you or keep it in your wallet. Write them down in several places if you're able so that you always have access to them and place them somewhere that you will see them so that you can read them aloud to yourself every day.

You should be reciting your affirmations/declarations to yourself at the very least 3 times per day (ideally much more than that). It's crucial that your affirmations/declarations are the first thing you say to yourself every morning.

ACHIEVEMENT TIP #9

Here are a few examples to get you started:

"I have more than enough time for everything that matters to me. There is an abundance of time in my day and I'm so grateful for it."

"I'm a magnet for money. More and more money flows to me effortlessly each day from a variety of places and for the great good of myself and others."

"I am capable and successful in achieving my goals."

One more thing about this topic of self talk – start to think of your brain as your greatest business partner. Your brain loves you and will always strive to prove you right. In other words, whatever you are telling it, it's going to try it's damnedest to prove you right. It will find ways to help you push through adversity and find new pathways to success.

ACHIEVEMENT TIP #10

Your brain doesn't recognize the negative, so make sure everything you say is in the positive (or in the "active" form).

For example, instead of saying "Don't lose." say "Win."

Instead of saying "Don't gain weight." say "Lose weight."

Instead of saying "Don't fail." say "Succeed."

This is a simple yet powerful habit that works to reframe your thought process. You will see a shift almost immediately.

You are a powerful force for good in this world. Go out and live the life of your dreams so that others may feel empowered to live the life of their dreams. Dedicate yourself to being a beacon of hope for others and an inspiration to everyone you meet.

Enjoy the Journey

Dear Soul-Searcher,

I hope that your adventure has been enlightening and inspiring. If you've taken the time to complete this book out and answer the questions honestly, you can consider it the heart-mind HQ. It's a place to return to when you're lost, when you're thinking of changing paths, or when you've lost motivation.

It's a guide that will always be there to answer questions for you and a place where change is possible through recognizing where you are and where you want to be.

But please recognize that, despite *you being the author of this journey*, this workbook is *not* the end-all-be-all for your life. Nothing in here is set in stone. This workbook, when filled with your truth, is meant to be a *compass*. It may point you in one cardinal direction, but you can always turn and go the other way. My hope for you is that this workbook *meets you where you are.*

What you answered today may not be what you truly want five years from now. People change – that is what keeps life invigorating. We search for different things and find out what we really desire through experimentation and discovery.

If you come back to this book and find that the answers no longer fill you with joy, don't feel the need to stick with them. There's *nothing wrong* with reworking your dreams. We are all on a branching path. Don't be afraid to start the entire process over to better serve you wherever you are.

If ever you have any questions about this workbook, feel free to email me at coachberta@dreamerssucceed.com

I'm happy to answer questions about the content or the work therein.

Before I go, I'd like to thank you for taking the time to read through this workbook. And don't forget to thank yourself for doing the hard work of self-discovery. In the end, it will bring you strength and guidance where you need it most.

Cheers to Success,

Berta Medina-Garcia

www.ingramcontent.com/pod-product-compliance
Lightning Source LLC
Chambersburg PA
CBHW050452110426
42744CB00013B/1968